SCIENCE & TECHNOLOGY

*Translated from the Italian
by Maureen Spurgeon*

© 2001 Istituto Geografico De Agostini, Novara
© 2002 Brown Watson, English edition
Reprinted 2003.

WHAT ARE ATOMS?

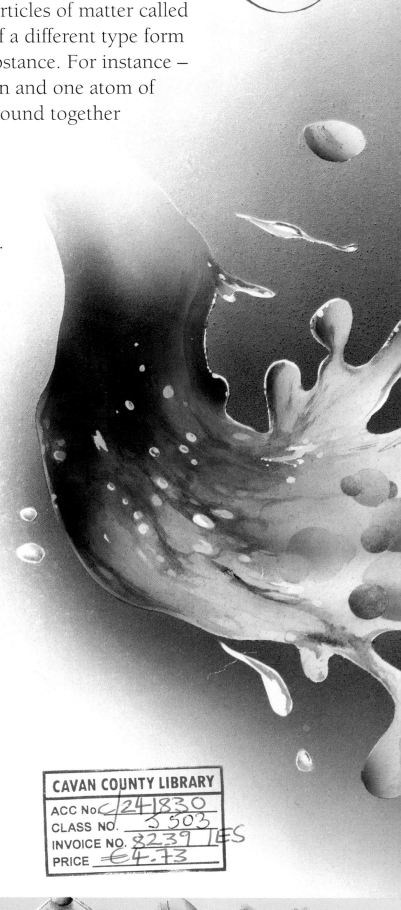

Everything around us is made up of tiny particles of matter called atoms. Two or more atoms of the same or of a different type form the molecule, which is the basis of each substance. For instance – a water molecule has two atoms of hydrogen and one atom of oxygen. Molecules of solid substances are bound together with a force which is very strong. The force which binds molecules of liquid is much weaker, and molecules in gases move in every direction. It was once thought that the atom was the smallest particle of matter. But scientists then discovered that atoms are made up of even smaller particles called electrons and protons, which each have an electrical charge. Electrons have a negative charge and move around the nucleus. Protons have a positive charge and are tied to the nucleus. Some atoms have neutrons which are also tied to the nucleus.

· HOW WHY WHEN ·

Why does iron go rusty?

Rust forms on the surfaces of iron objects when they are exposed to the air. It is the product of a chemical reaction called oxydization. The more the object is exposed to the air, the more rapidly rust spreads. Once rust has formed, it makes the surface crumble, exposing the layers underneath to the air so that these too become rusty as a result of oxydization.

ORGANIC AND INORGANIC CHEMISTRY

Organic chemistry is the study carbon compounds. Carbon is one of the basic elements of living organisms. Inorganic chemistry is the study of chemical compounds.

- There are actually more than 200 sub-atomic particles.
- One grain of dust contains a billion atoms.
- One drop of water contains 10 billion water molecules.
- One molecule of hydrogen contains two atoms of hydrogen.

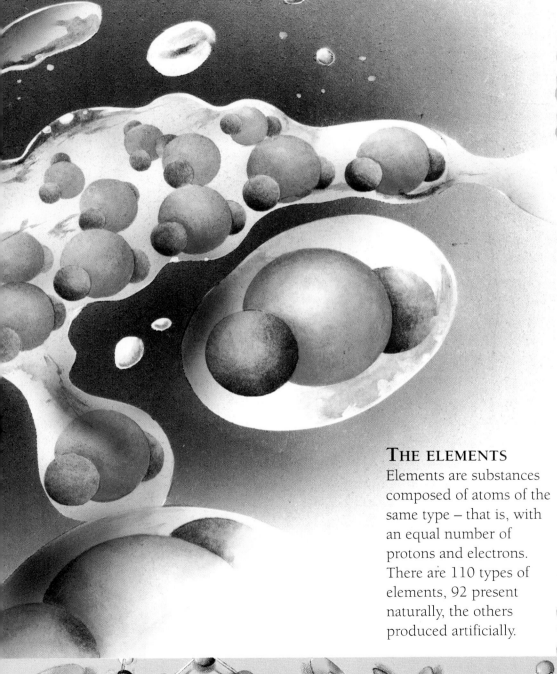

WHY DOES A SLICED APPLE GO BROWN AFTER A WHILE?

A chemical reaction can separate, unite or combine differently the elements which constitute a substance. A simple contact between two molecules can be enough for a chemical reaction. Other times it happens by the intervention of heat or electricity, or by a catalyst (an external factor which activates the reaction). In chemical reactions, matter is transformed, but not destroyed, nor is new matter created. A sliced apple goes brown due to the chemical reaction of oxydization – because the iron content in the apple combines with oxygen in the air.

THE ELEMENTS

Elements are substances composed of atoms of the same type – that is, with an equal number of protons and electrons. There are 110 types of elements, 92 present naturally, the others produced artificially.

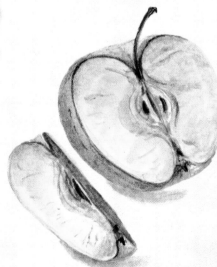

WHAT MAKES A FLAME?

A flame is a bright, shining mixture generated by the combustion (burning) of a substance, either solid, liquid or gas. For a flame to burn, there must be three elements – 1) heat; 2) the combustive (oxygen); and 3) the combustible (a material such as wax or petrol, which can be burned). A match bursts into flame when the 'head' is at the right temperature for the oxygen to burn the sulphur. When we blow on the match, we reduce the temperature and so the combustion is interrupted.

THE REMAINS OF COMBUSTION

Smoke, cinders and soot are among the products of combustion. When a substance burns, it is not completely destroyed but is transformed into other substances and into heat.

• HOW WHY WHEN •

How do we measure the temperature of something?

There are many scales for measuring temperature, each one named after its inventor – Celsius, Fahrenheit, Kelvin and Rankine. The one commonly used in most countries is the Celsius Scale (C). Here are some examples:

250°C: temperature of the combustion of wood

100°C: temperature of boiling water

37°C: normal body temperature of a human

0°C: temperature of frozen water

-39°C: temperature of solidification of mercury

-273°C: absolute zero (complete absence of heat).

THE SHAPE OF A FLAME

A flame has an elongated shape, because the hot air is lighter than the cold air, and so the hot air rises upwards.

Try this simple experiment to prove that a flame goes out without oxygen. Take a candle and fix to a plate with a little piece of modelling clay. With the help of an adult, light the candle, then cover it with a glass jar. In a few moments, you will see the flame going out, because the oxygen in the jar will be used up.

WHAT IS COMBUSTIBLE?

Substances which burn rapidly in the presence of oxygen and which give off large quantities of heat are called combustibles. Such substances are used to produce light, heat and energy. Combustible solids include firewood and coal. Benzine, gasoline and kerosene are all derived from petrol, a liquid combustible. Natural gas and methane are combustible gases.

WHY DOES LIGHTNING STRIKE?

Spectacular flashes of lightning are caused by short, violent transfers of electric charges, either between one cloud and another, or between clouds and the earth. During a thunderstorm, the lower parts of clouds (the parts nearest the earth) accumulate lots of negative electric charges – whilst, on the ground, positive electric charges accumulate. When there is a build-up of negative charges in the sky, these charges move towards the positive charges on the earth, and cause lightning. This in turn causes a further exchange of positive charges from the earth. What happens then is that the negative electric charges jump towards the upper parts of the cloud, which is when we see the lightning flashing upwards.

● HOW WHY WHEN WHO ●

Who invented the lightning conductor?

The Lightning Conductor was invented by the American Benjamin Franklin in 1752. He built a kite with an iron tip, threaded a key (also of iron) at the bottom of the string, and flew the kite during a thunderstorm. Franklin proved that the iron tip attracted the lightning and carried the electric charge down the string to the key – in fact, Franklin got an electric shock by touching the key. Following the experiment, Franklin built his first Lightning Conductor, a steel mast which he placed a short distance from his house. The point of this Lightning Conductor attracted the stormy electric charges and dispersed these into the ground, avoiding any damage caused by lightning striking the building.

ATTRACTION
Opposite electric charges attract. Charges of the same repel. During a storm, the positive charges on the ground attract the negative charges in the clouds.

CHARGES IN MOVEMENT

Positive electric charges are enclosed within the nucleus, and so cannot move. Negative charges are outside the nucleus and so can be overcome or acquired. The atoms which are overcome remain with a larger number of positive charges. Those which are acquired will remain with more negative charges.

When something becomes electrified, it acquires the capacity to attract lightweight objects, acting rather like a magnet. To prove this, stroke a balloon with a piece of wool. The electrons of the wool pass on to the balloon. On the wool there will be positive charges and, because opposite charges attract, the wool and the balloon are drawn together. Now tie two inflated balloons at either end of a length of thread. Stroke a piece of wool on the balloons and hold the thread in the centre. You will see that the balloons draw apart, because they have taken the same type of (negative) charges from the piece of wool.

ELECTRIC CHARGES

Atoms are formed by some particles with negative electric charges and others with positive charges. When there is an equal number of charges, the atom is neutral.

IS IT POSSIBLE TO ELECTRIFY AN OBJECT?

An object can be electrified by stroking it with a different material. For instance, a glass rod can be electrified by stroking it with wool. A moving car 'strokes' against the air and becomes charged with electricity. This phenomenon is temporary, because the electrical charges which accumulate are dispersed on contact with other objects. Have you ever seen little 'sparks' coming from your hair when you pull a sweater over your head? Or felt a tiny electrical shock by taking the hand of another person, or touching a car door? All these happen due to a sudden transfer of electrons from one electrified object to another – like flashes of lightning!

WHY DOES A LIGHT BULB GET HOT?

Light shines from an electric bulb because of the tungsten element inside it. The electricity enters the bulb along a filament, goes around the tungsten spiral and out through another filament. Tungsten is a metal conductor of electricity. But the spiral is so thin that it is hard for the electric current to pass through it. The force needed heats the tungsten spiral to the point where it results in light. And so the bulb gives off light and heat at the same time.

HOW DOES A TOASTER WORK?

Many things used in the home transform electrical energy into heat energy. Inside a toaster there are metal filaments, similar to those inside a light bulb. These heat up with the passage of an electrical current and so transform the electrical energy into heat. There are many other things which work in the same way – electric blankets, irons, hair-dryers and electric cookers.

• HOW WHY WHEN •

Does electricity always produce heat?

In some cases, the heat produced by electricity is a problem, because it causes the dispersal and waste of part of the energy. Scientists have discovered that some metals, when cooled, do not resist the passage of the current, and so do not transform any of the electricity into heat. These metals called 'superconductors' are now widely used – for instance, in the construction of railway lines carrying high speed trains.

WHAT HAPPENS INSIDE AN ELECTRIC CABLE?

Electrical cables are 'canals' along which the current flows, connecting the different components of a circuit. Inside a cable there are thin filaments of copper which conduct the electricity. Copper, like other metals, has electrons which are free to move and therefore able to carry electricity from one point of the cable to another. Electrical cables are covered with plastic, a material that does not allow electricity to flow through. So we can touch the plastic covering of a cable without getting a shock.

HOW DO BATTERIES MAKE A RADIO WORK?

Batteries are like little supplies of electrical energy. Inside there is a chemical substance which can transform chemical energy into electrical energy. When we turn on a radio, the metal cap of the battery comes into contact with certain metal parts of the equipment; or, the internal composition of the battery creates a flow of electrons which generates the current. A battery is 'dead' when the composition inside is used up.

● HOW WHY WHAT WHEN ●

What is an electric current?

An electric current is a passage of electrons from one electrified body to another which is less charged. When too many electrons are generated, they can move. For example – when we work a light switch, or switch an electrical gadget on or off, we release some of the electricity stored in the central installation in the house, making it flow along the filaments until it reaches the gadget, or the light bulb.

WHY DO TWO MAGNETS SOMETIMES PUSH APART FROM EACH OTHER?

The two ends of a magnet are called poles. Each pole has a different electric charge (positive and negative). The positive pole of a magnet is always attracted to the negative pole of another magnet. But if two poles of the same charge are put near each other, the magnets push apart with a force of repulsion which can never be overcome.

MAGLEV TRAINS

Maglev (Magnetic Levitation) trains travel centimetres above the rails – because, instead of wheels, they have a system of magnets worked by electricity, the same as the rails. So as the same magnetic poles are pulled towards each other, they constantly repel (push apart).

• HOW WHY WHEN •

Why does the needle of a compass always point to the North?

The Earth is like a giant magnet. Its poles (North and South) produce a magnetic field which makes anything magnetic and movable point towards them. It is believed that this phenomenon is due to the steel and nickel in the nucleus of the Earth and also the rotation of the Earth which causes the rotation of the compass needle. The geographical North Pole and South Pole are not the same as the Earth's magnetic poles. In fact, the magnetic poles are some thousands of kilometres away from the geographical poles.

To magnetize a needle, find a bar magnet and two large needles. Stroke the magnet along each needle 40 times, always in the same direction. Then push one needle towards the other, first by the eye, then by the point. You will see that the needles act like two magnets, pulling together or pushing apart, according to which ends of the needles meet.

HOW DOES THE MAGNETIC COMPASS WORK?

A magnetic needle is fixed at the centre of a magnetic compass, on a pivot, so that it can rotate freely. The four cardinal points (north, south, east and west) are shown on the face, with the other geographical points in between. The needle always points to the magnetic North Pole, so that the other cardinal points can be calculated.

WHY DOES A ROLLING BALL GO DOWNWARDS?

If a ball is placed on a flat surface, it will only move by means of an external force – such as a kick or a gust of wind. But if the ball is placed on a slope, it will roll towards the bottom, moved by the force of gravity. If we roll a ball across a flat surface, we will see it slowing down after a while. This is because another force intervenes – friction against the ground, which slows down the movement of the ball until it stops. The friction comes from the contact between the surface of the ball and that of the flat surface.

TO 'HOLD' THE ROAD

If a car or bicycle were to go along on smooth tyres, they would not be able to 'hold' the road. The grooves in the rubber, that is, the 'tread', create a good friction with the asphalt and therefore enable the vehicles to 'hold' the road during curves and when braking.

TO TRAVEL FASTER

Although friction controls movement, in some cases it can reduce speed. That is why aircraft and speed-boats have pointed shapes, in order to reduce friction with the air and water and to travel at high speeds.

• HOW WHY WHEN •

Why does a sudden braking throw us forward?

When any method of transport stops suddenly, the passengers are thrown forward, as if they were still going on. If the transport starts suddenly, the passengers are 'pulled' back, as if they were wanting to remain still. Each body tends to remain inert – that is, to remain in the state in which it began. Therefore, it reacts in a manner contrary to the stimulus which changed its original state.

WHY CAN'T A BABY STAND ON ITS FEET?

If you have ever managed to balance a pen on your finger, you will have discovered its centre of gravity – that is, its point of balance. But if you move the centre of balance away, then the pen falls. In the human body, the centre of gravity is situated more or less under the tummy button. To remain in relation to our centre of gravity, our body is balanced on our feet, otherwise we cannot stand unaided. Small babies cannot stand on their feet because they cannot support their body weight and achieve the right balance.

WHY DO OUTSTRETCHED ARMS HELP BALANCE?

By stretching out the arms, the balance of the body is distributed differently and the centre of gravity remains above the base of support. Try getting up from a chair, keeping your feet in front of it and your arms by your sides. You will not be able to do it! But if you put your feet under the chair and move your arms forward, you will focus your centre of gravity on your feet once more and this will enable you to keep your balance and stand up.

• HOW WHY WHEN •

Why do all cars have their engines mounted at the bottom?

To avoid becoming overturned easily, all vehicles are built in such a way that the centre of gravity is between the wheels. That is why the engine, the heaviest part of the car, is always at the bottom. If this weight were at the top of the vehicle, its balance would be at risk with each curve.

WHY DOES A ROAD RISING UPWARD HAVE LOTS OF CURVES?

To climb to the top of a mountain along a straight path, a mountaineer would need great physical strength. Also for cars, the force needed would be enormous. The curves in a mountain road make the journey longer, but they reduce not only the hard work of the climb but also the speed of ascent. So the winding road reduces the force necessary to complete a task. Tools which do the same are called simple machines.

SLOPING SURFACES

The curving road and the spiral staircase each reduces the force necessary to reach a height. In this way, they can be compared to simple machines.

• HOW WHY WHEN •

How does a pulley work?

The pulley is a simple device which enables great weights to be lifted. It comprises a grooved disc or pulley which spins on a pivot fixed to a stirrup, around which passes a rope or a chain. At one end of the rope is fixed the item to be lifted, at the other is the person applying the force. To make the pulley work, a person uses his or her weight, pulling one end of the rope towards the ground, so that the weight rises up at the other end.

SCREWS

Imagine that the thread of a screw is a sloping surface. The screw penetrates into a surface with a spiral course, rising up vertically.

1) *Which tool simplifies the job of pulling a splinter from a finger?*

2) *Which simple tool consists of rotating wheels with teeth?*

3) *To raise the lid of a can, is it best to lever it off with a coin or with a screwdriver?*

4) *What is the positioning point of a lever called?*

Answers
1) tweezers 2) gear 3) screwdriver 4) pivot

FORCE MULTIPLIERS

A force multiplier is a simple machine which multiplies a small amount of human strength in order to move a load.

The corkscrew increases the strength of our hands. We can pull a cork out of a bottle, by pushing down the arms of the corkscrew.

The car jack enables a person to lift a car.

A crowbar is used to force open structures and objects which are stiff and resistant.

Nut-crackers do a job which would be too difficult for pure muscular strength.

All these simple machines are examples of force multipliers.

WHY IS A RAINBOW COLOURED?

The light from the Sun may appear white to us. But it actually consists of seven colours. If a beam of light crosses through the drops of water which remain suspended in the air after rainfall, it splits up into its seven colours and we see a rainbow in the sky. The same composition can be seen by making a beam of light pass through a glass prism. The colours of the rainbow always appear in the same order – red, orange, yellow, green, blue, indigo and violet.

ISAAC NEWTON

It was the English scientist Isaac Newton (1642-1727) who discovered that when crossing through a triangular prism of glass, 'white' light is split up into different colours.

● HOW WHY WHEN WHO ●

Who invented the telescope?

The telescope is an instrument in which a concave mirror gathers in the light at one point called the objective, to produce an enlarged image. The first telescope was invented in Holland in 1608 by Hans Lippershey. Galileo improved on this and in 1609 built the first telescope to study the sky. This was made from a tube with a lens at each end. Modern telescopes owe their origin to the invention of the first reflective telescope by Isaac Newton (1668) which used mirrors in place of lenses, obtaining sharper images.

HOW DO LENSES CHANGE IMAGES?

The surface of lenses are curved. Therefore, they bend the rays of light which pass through them. Convex lenses make rays of light converge at one point. Concave lenses make rays of light spread out.

• The largest space telescope is the Hubble Space Telescope, put into orbit by a Space Shuttle in 1990. It has a mirror 24m in diameter weighing 11 tonnes.

• The smallest optical prism was made in a scientific laboratory in Colorado, USA, and is almost invisible, measuring 0.01mm.

• A normal microscope (with lenses and mirrors) can enlarge an element up to 2000 times, an electronic microscope more than one million times.

REFRACTION
The way in which a beam of light passing through a substance changes direction is called refraction. In the case of a rainbow, the light passes through raindrops, seeming to make the colours bend in the sky.

Convex and concave lenses are used in the manufacture of spectacles and other optical instruments, such as photographic machines, microscopes, projectors, binoculars and telescopes.

Rays of light, when they undergo refraction by a lens, create an enlarged or smaller image. Lenses used to examine small things, such as insects or postage stamps are convex.

WHAT IS A LASER?

A laser is a device which can generate a beam of light which is very fine and intense and can concentrate a large quantity of energy at one point. With its power and precision, the laser is now widely used for many tasks – cutting sheets of steel, welding metals, carrying out delicate operations in surgery, creating spectacular lighting effects in the sky, producing and reading compact discs, reading bar codes on products and many more.

• HOW WHY WHAT WHEN •

What is a bank card?

A bank card is a magnetic pass stamped with the automatic code of the bank. Memorized in a magnetic strip on the pass is a small electronic circuit and usually, sometimes also in bar code, personal details of the owner, their secret code (PIN/Personal Identification Number) and details of the person's bank account. All this is fed to the withdrawal computer which then delivers the bank-notes to the cash dispenser and deducts the sum from the account.

WHY IS THERE A BAR CODE ON THINGS THAT WE BUY?

In most shops, all the information about a product (quantity in a packet, trade name, content, etc.) are memorized and processed by computer. The bar code contains information on the brand, the type of product, the contents and which elements distinguish the product from others which are similar. Price is not usually indicated, because this can change. When the bar code is seen by a laser scanner, this 'translates' the black and white bars into information. The white stripes reflect the light of the laser, the scanner transforms the light impulse into an electrical impulse and transmits this to a computer.

How does a compact disc contain sound?

The surface of a compact disc is aluminium, coated in transparent plastic. The metal disc underneath has grooves scored by a laser. Each groove is made up of microsocopic 'dots' which have a digital code representing the sounds. When we insert a CD into a player, a low-power laser beam is directed on to the rotating disc. The grooves and the flat parts on the surface reflect the light in different ways, creating a particular sequence of light impulses which are then read by a sensor and transformed into sound.

FACTS·AND·FIGURES

• According to type, the DVD can have a capacity of memory which is equal to 7, 14 or 26 CDs.

• A CD-ROM (read only) is used to load data into a computer. It has a memory equal to that of 400 floppy disks of 1.44MB.

• The diameter of a CD is 12cm.

• A DVD can read at a speed of 30 times more than that of a CD.

WHAT IS A DVD?

DVD stands for *Digital Versatile Disc*. It looks rather like a compact disc, but can contain a far larger quantity of data and can read at a much faster speed. One DVD video can input between two to eight hours of images and sound at the highest definition. One DVD can contain the original version of a film, different versions in other languages or with sub-titles.

WHAT ARE FIBRE OPTICS?

Fibre optics are very fine filaments of transparent glass covered with a plastic material which makes them flexible and resistant. They are used to illuminate and to observe places which are not easily reached (inside the human body, for example) or to transmit coded information in the form of light signals (for example, in telephonic network or in those televised via cable). Due to the high speed of transmission (approximately two or three times the speed of light) and the ability to transfer a remarkable volume of information, fibre optics are the method of communication for the future.

FIBRE OPTICS AND MEDICINE

Fibre optics are used to look inside the human body. Because they are so fine and flexible, they can reach parts of the body which could not otherwise be reached without surgery. Fibre optics can illuminate a part of the body and transmit images to the doctor who can see these on a separate, external screen.

● HOW WHY WHAT WHEN ●

What is a mirage?

Rays of light also undergo a distortion when they pass from warm air to cold air, or vice versa, because of their different density. On very hot days, the air near the ground heats up very quickly, and the rays of light which pass through the hot air become distorted. That is why to our eyes the road appears damp – but, in fact, we are seeing the reflection of the sky. This type of reflection can also make something appear to be upside down, or create the illusion of a mirror image of a reflection of water. This phenomenon is called a mirage.

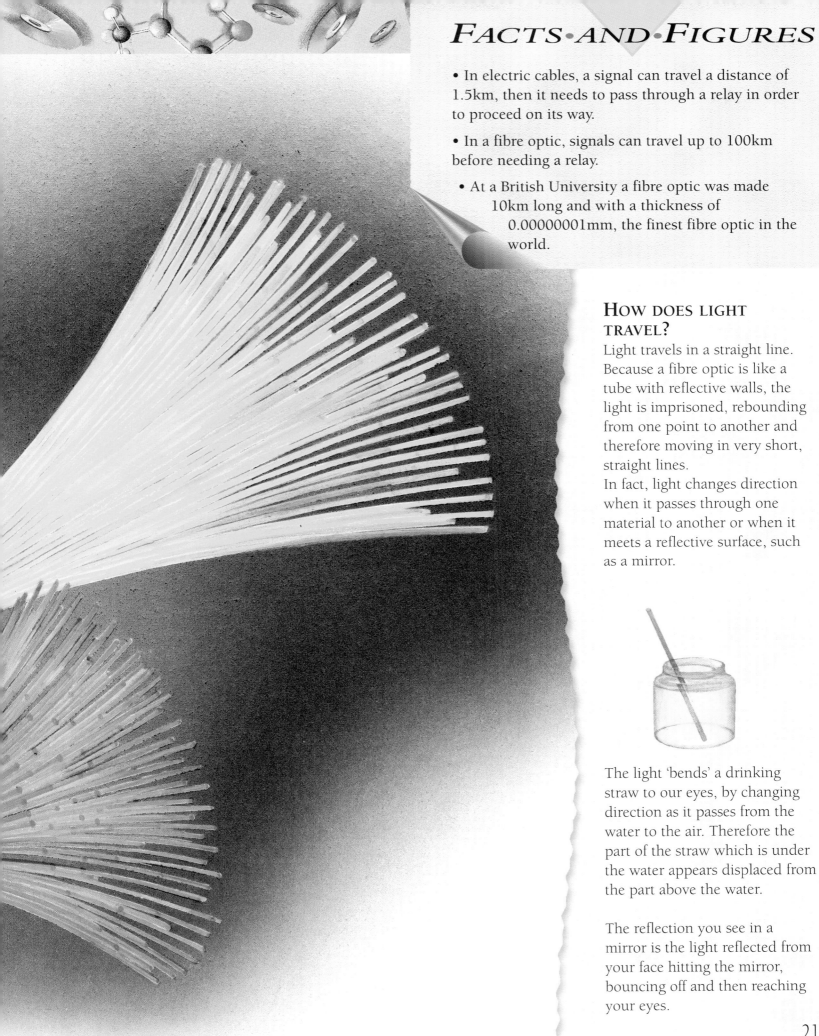

FACTS·AND·FIGURES

- In electric cables, a signal can travel a distance of 1.5km, then it needs to pass through a relay in order to proceed on its way.

- In a fibre optic, signals can travel up to 100km before needing a relay.

- At a British University a fibre optic was made 10km long and with a thickness of 0.00000001mm, the finest fibre optic in the world.

HOW DOES LIGHT TRAVEL?

Light travels in a straight line. Because a fibre optic is like a tube with reflective walls, the light is imprisoned, rebounding from one point to another and therefore moving in very short, straight lines.
In fact, light changes direction when it passes through one material to another or when it meets a reflective surface, such as a mirror.

The light 'bends' a drinking straw to our eyes, by changing direction as it passes from the water to the air. Therefore the part of the straw which is under the water appears displaced from the part above the water.

The reflection you see in a mirror is the light reflected from your face hitting the mirror, bouncing off and then reaching your eyes.

WHY CAN'T AN AEROPLANE STOP IN MID-FLIGHT?

When an aeroplane flies into the sky pushed by the force of its engines, the air flows rapidly over its wings. Beneath the wings, the air slows down, because of the way the wings are curved. This creates a different force of pressure on the underside of the wing, which results in an upward push to sustain the aircraft. This upward thrust is called 'lift'. If the aircraft had to stop in flight, it would cancel out this difference in force between the air above the wing and the air below and the aircraft would crash.

REFUELLING IN THE AIR
Because aircraft cannot stop in the air, fuel tanks must be refilled whilst flying. This is especially important in particular situations, such as war, when aircraft cannot refuel on enemy territory and so have to cover long distances without stopping.

THINGS·TO·DO

Cut a strip of thin paper, about 10cm x 20cm. Hold it beneath your lips, and blow on the top surface. You will see that the paper does not bend down as you blow, but rises up. This is because the air flowing across the upper part of the strip exerts a lesser pressure than that which is exerted by the surrounding air. It is this pressure which makes the paper rise up – just like the air supporting the wings of aircraft.

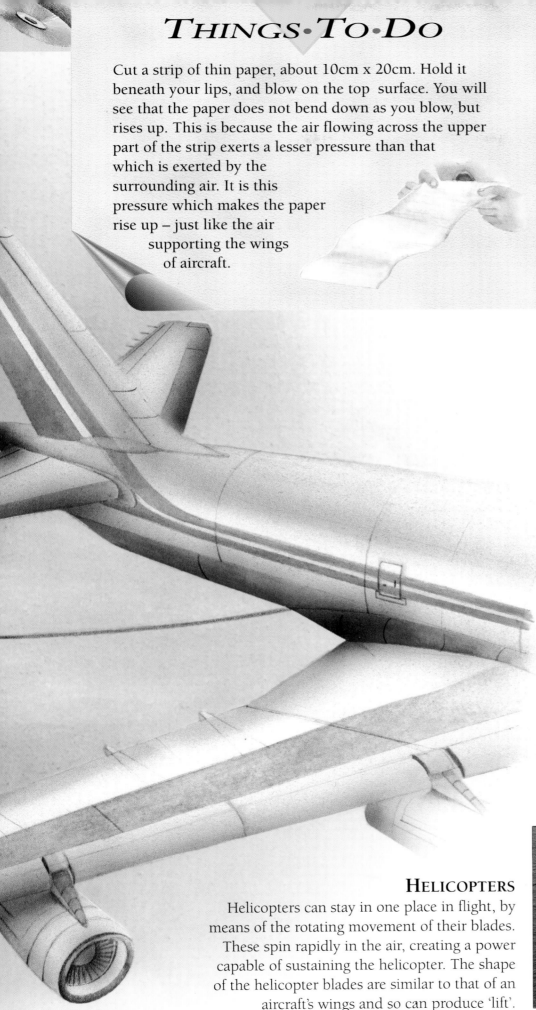

WHAT WILL THE AIRCRAFT OF THE FUTURE BE LIKE?

Scientists predict that the aircraft of the future will have supersonic speeds. It will be possible to fly from Rome to Los Angeles in less than 4 hours, instead of the 10 hours flying-time today. There will also be new solutions for the comfort and safety of passengers. Aircraft of the future will have an increasing number of instruments for the prevention of accidents. It will also be possible to pilot an aircraft to the ground using new and sophisticated communication technology, thus eliminating the 'human factor' which can sometimes put aircraft safety at risk.

HELICOPTERS

Helicopters can stay in one place in flight, by means of the rotating movement of their blades. These spin rapidly in the air, creating a power capable of sustaining the helicopter. The shape of the helicopter blades are similar to that of an aircraft's wings and so can produce 'lift'.

HOW DO SUBMARINES RISE TO THE SURFACE?

Submarines reach the depths of the oceans by filling tanks with water. When they want to surface, this water is let out of the tanks and replaced by compressed air. These two operations allow the submarine to vary the level of immersion by the quantity of air present in the tanks.

• HOW WHY WHEN •

How is it that ships float?

An object immersed in water receives an upward thrust, equal to the weight of the water that object moves. This is called the Archimedes Principle. Because of their shape, ships move enormous quantities of water and so receive an upward thrust sufficient to make them float. But staying afloat also depends on a material's density – that is, the relationship between its weight and its volume. A ship is built of dense materials, like steel, but inside there are hollow cavities, full of air. These make the density of the ship less than that of the water, and so it keeps afloat.

WILL IT BE POSSIBLE TO LIVE AT THE BOTTOM OF THE SEA?

There are architects and town planners who are studying the possibility of installing underwater bases and laboratories, connected to the surface by a complex system of cables.

- The fastest speed recorded by a craft at sea is that reached by a USA war hovercraft SES-100B at 170km per hour.

- USA nuclear submarines have been designed to cover distances of 640,000km without being refuelled.

- The largest sailing ship is the *Sedov*, in the service of the Russian Navy. It is 109m long and 14.6m wide.

DOUBLE HULL

The hull of a submarine is usually double – the internal hull to withstand the pressure of water; the external hull has a shape perfect for navigation.

Before the dream of people living under the oceans can become a reality, solutions will need to be found to overcome problems such as isolation, climate and lack of sunlight so that people can live happily and safely whilst being able to explore their surroundings.

HOW DOES A VIDEO GAME WORK?

Every day, when we use the radio, the television, the computer or when we go into a shop with an automatic door, we put various electronic devices into action. Inside hand-held video games are miniaturized gadgets. The electric current does not flow constantly through these, as in an ordinary piece of electronic equipment, but is modified in signals. The video game transforms the mechanical signal (the touch from your finger), into a magnetic signal which makes it follow another on the screen (the images on display) in a continuous succession of signals going in and coming out.

ELECTRONIC CIRCUITS

Electronic circuits have components such as resistors, condensers, diodes and transistors. A single circuit can contain hundreds of miniaturized components which regulate the way in which the electricity is used. These components can amplify, activate, de-activate or turn off the equipment.

● HOW WHY WHAT WHEN ●

What is the 'language' of micro-chips?

The 'language' of the micro-chip is the binary code, which comprises just two signals, 'on' and 'off', which is translated as '1' and '0' like an alphabet of only two letters. Each piece of information which is entered into a chip, whether it is a sound, a drawing or a word, is converted into this code.

WHAT IS A MICRO-CHIP?

A micro-chip is truly microscopic in size – just a few square millimetres. But it is a complex electronic gadget capable of carrying out numerous and complicated functions inside televisions, telephones, computers. The micro-chip is mounted on a tiny, thin layer of silicone, which is a semi-conductive material, enclosed in a rigid, protective covering and connected to the equipment by little 'feet'.

One piece of electronic equipment can use numerous micro-chips, each with a specific function. In a telephone, for example, one micro-chip has the job of memorizing telephone numbers. Another records messages, others generate messages to appear on a screen, or transform signals into sound. The more electronic components in a chip, the more powerful and faster the equipment.

WHERE CAN WE USE A COMPUTER?

The constant development of communication systems has led to many of us taking part in debates by computer and playing games with people far away. We only have to go into a library or internet café to send electronic messages almost anywhere in the world. By way of a telephone line, the computers, connected together, form small and large networks. A school network allows all students to use the same information through different computers. The Internet connects computers worldwide, reducing distances between people and allowing the exchange of an enormous amount of information.

WWW

This means World Wide Web and indicates the multimedia system of information which can be accessed via the Internet – that is, across a network of computers connected on a world level.

● HOW WHY WHAT WHEN ●

What is a video conference?

People far apart can 'meet together' to discuss topics concerning their work, or to study whilst remaining seated in front of the computer. Images and sounds can be transmitted by tiny tele-cameras and microphones placed on top of the computer monitor of each person taking part, so that everyone can see who is speaking.

FACTS·AND·FIGURES

- In 1995, there were 5 million computers connected to the Internet. At the end of 1998, it was more than 100 million – but this number is continually increasing and in the next few years, a 'growth explosion' is forecast.
- The USA is the country with the highest number of subscribers connected to the Internet – more than 50% of the total population.
- Sales of the Microsoft Flight Simulator game have exceeded 21 million copies.

WHAT IS VIRTUAL REALITY?

Virtual reality is a 3-dimensional environment, constructed electronically by computer. The user enters into the environment by wearing a helmet equipped with visualizers over the eyes. Computer-created images and sounds give users the sensation of actually moving within the place they see. The technology of virtual reality can be used not only in leisure (e.g. interactive video games) but also for professional purposes. For instance – doctors can gain experience of difficult surgical operations before they actually do them; pilots can carry out an emergency landing without risk, thanks to simulated flying practice. Architects can 'enter' a stately home, or illustrate a project before it is built. The gadgets to access any virtual surroundings can even be connected into the hands of a subscriber (by means of a special 'data glove') or to the whole body, by a special overall.

THE BIRTH OF THE INTERNET

The system of connecting computers on a network was developed for military purposes in 1969, by the Department of Defence of the USA. Then it extended into large corporations and research organizations. Today, millions of people worldwide are connected to the Internet.

CAN ROBOTS THINK?

Robots are automatic machines which can help people to do complex and repetitive tasks. A robot can work through a computer which is already programmed, but cannot work independently. There have been studies and research with the aim of developing the robot's ability to interact with its surroundings. Some robots can already adapt their work with a reduced number of external stimuli. Although there will never be a robot which can 'think', some can react to unexpected stimuli and interact with people.

• HOW WHEN WHY •

How does a robot work?

Until now, no robot can function independently. It must always depend on the external control of a person. There are three phases in the function of a robot : 1) an external computer gives the instructions; 2) a motor makes the robot move; 3) other internal gadgets, called sensors, regulate and correct the robot's movements. There are some robots guided by a person, and which, in an environment of virtual reality, can simulate the actions necessary and transmit them.

WHAT CAN A ROBOT DO?

Robots are widely used in industry to help people in jobs which are tiring, dangerous and which need particular precision. In the car industry, robots cut and weld bodywork parts, or varnish different pieces. In the electronics industry, a robot can assemble different components.

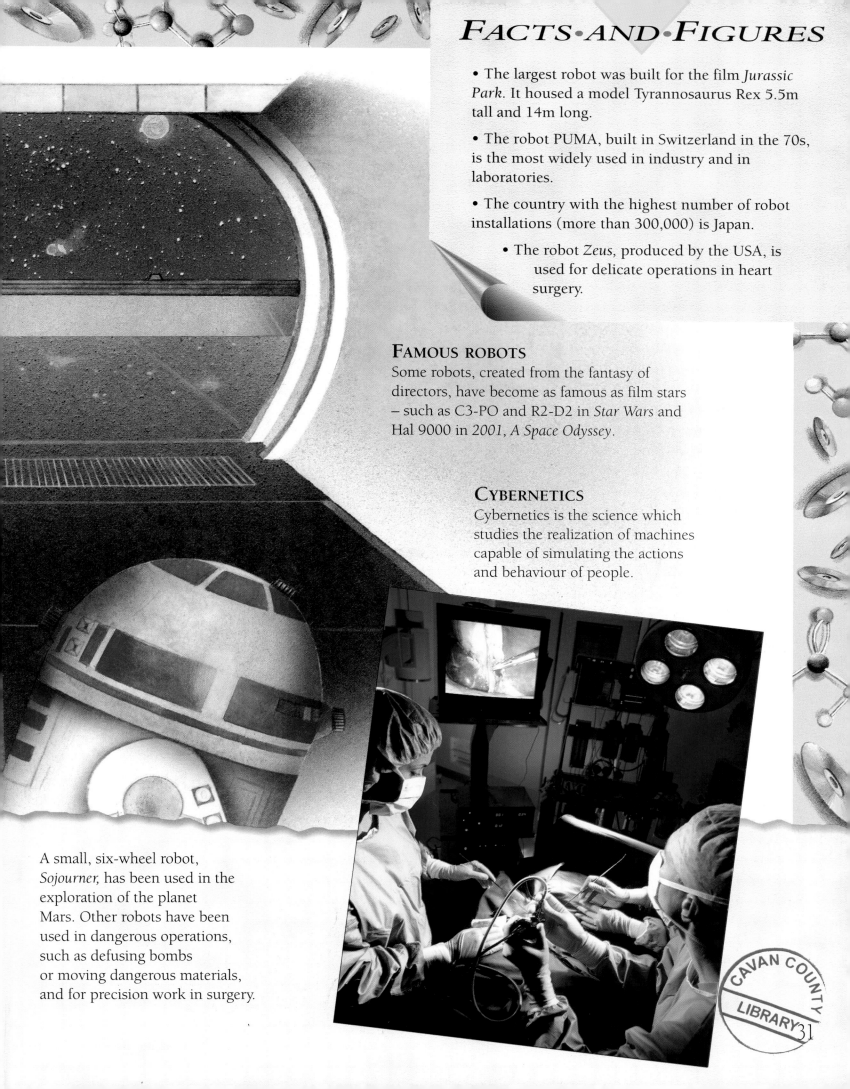

- The largest robot was built for the film *Jurassic Park*. It housed a model Tyrannosaurus Rex 5.5m tall and 14m long.

- The robot PUMA, built in Switzerland in the 70s, is the most widely used in industry and in laboratories.

- The country with the highest number of robot installations (more than 300,000) is Japan.

- The robot *Zeus*, produced by the USA, is used for delicate operations in heart surgery.

FAMOUS ROBOTS

Some robots, created from the fantasy of directors, have become as famous as film stars – such as C3-PO and R2-D2 in *Star Wars* and Hal 9000 in *2001, A Space Odyssey*.

CYBERNETICS

Cybernetics is the science which studies the realization of machines capable of simulating the actions and behaviour of people.

A small, six-wheel robot, *Sojourner,* has been used in the exploration of the planet Mars. Other robots have been used in dangerous operations, such as defusing bombs or moving dangerous materials, and for precision work in surgery.

INDEX